My Precious Gift

Written By
Yekatit Bezooayehu

Illustrations by
Whimsical Designs by CJ

This book is dedicated to my mom and dad.

My Precious Gift © Yekatit Bezooayehu
Illustrations by Whimsical Designs by CJ

All rights reserved. No part of this book may be reproduced, transmitted, or stored in an information retrieval system in any form or by any means, graphic, electronic, or mechanical, including photocopying, taping, and recording, without prior written permission from the author.

First Printing, 2021

Printed in the United States of America

ISBN: 978-0-578-86873-8

When I was born, mom and dad gave me a spectacular *gift*.

This *gift* shows who I am and where I come from.

This *gift* makes me proud of where I come from because it has a very rich history.

Because of this *gift*, I am part of a unique culture that has extraordinary customs and great traditions.

Each part of my family's heritage makes me one of a kind.

We wear *beautiful* handmade clothes.

We listen to songs and dance to tribal music.

We speak in our native language.

Do you want to know what the *gift* is?

My precious *gift* is my name.
My name is magical and powerful.
I carry it wherever I go.

Sometimes people laugh because my name sounds different and is hard to say.

But I always smile and help them speak my gift.

My friends ask,
"can we give you an easier name?"

I tell them no because they will miss the great meaning of my name.

THE END.

NAME

My Precious Gift

What does your name mean?

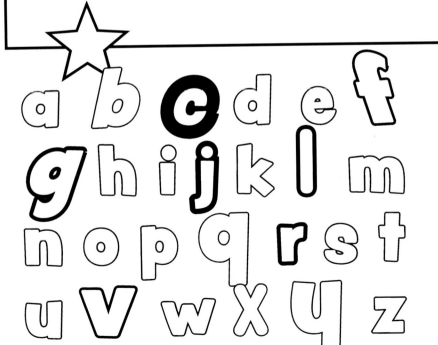

Write the first letter of your name as a capital letter.

About the Author

Yekatit Bezooayehu is a lifelong educator, community servant, and lover of all things creative arts. Her first children's story is a homage to her deep East African culture and history. Yekatit is the only child born to immigrant parents from Addis Abba, Ethiopia. When choosing a name, her parents wanted to honor the legacy of their great motherland. The direct translation of her name from Amharic to English is first name "February" and last name "I have seen a lot." As a child growing up in America, Yekatit recalls feeling ashamed of her name because she was often teased for the difficulty in pronunciation. She even went so far as to ask her parents for a name change; good thing they never gave in to her request. As she got older, Yekatit was able to fully embrace and deeply appreciate her given treasure. She passionately believes that this story will inspire children to be inquisitive about their family history, cultural traditions and embrace how those things makes them exceptionally unique, one of a kind, and unlike anyone else. Yekatit was born in Washington, DC, raised in Houston, Texas and now lives in Maryland with her mom and very spoiled fur baby, King Carlos.

I Love My...

Draw 6 things you love about yourself.

Made in the USA
Middletown, DE
22 September 2021